THE PEACE AND PLENTY

Journal of Well-Spent Moments

SARAH BAN BREATHNACH

I would like to gratefully acknowledge all of the writers I have quoted for their wisdom, comfort and inspiration. An exhaustive search was undertaken to determine whether previously published material included in this book required permission to reprint or be quoted. If there has been an error, I deeply apologize and a correction will be made in subsequent editions.

The legal and moral rights of Sarah Ban Breathnach to be identified as the author of this work and the creator of the intellectual property concepts contained within, including Simple Abundance®, "Gratitude Journal," Illustrated Discovery Journal," *The Peace and Plenty Journal of Well-Spent Moments*™, *The Peace and Plenty Comfort Companion*™, and The Thrill of Thrift™ has been asserted.

Simple Abundance® is a registered trademark of Simple Abundance, Inc and used by Simple Abundance Press with permission.

Cover design and Peace and Plenty acorn illustration by Patrick Munger ©Simple Abundance, Inc. 2010

Simple Abundance Press
P.O. Box 4296
Redondo Beach, CA 90277
www.simpleabundance.com
www.simpleabundancepress.net

Printed in the United States

10 9 8 7 6 5 4 3 2 1

ISBN-978-0-9817809-3-1

The
Peace and Plenty
Journal of
Well-Spent
Moments

Sarah Ban Breathnach

Simple Abundance Press

Upon Creating a Journal of Well-Spent Moments

You are discontented with the world because you
just can't get the small things that suit your pleasure.
--George Eliot

Welcome to the *Peace and Plenty Journal of Well-Spent Moments*, your private numbered account, a compilation of wisdom and wealth that the world cannot take away.

The practice of Gratitude in our lives doesn't require us to stay stuck in misery, lack or denial. Instead, Gratitude asks us to knowledge and accept the reality of our situation so that we can get our spiritual bearings. If you're experiencing difficult financial circumstances, whether this is sudden or new to you or has been going on for a long time, it's very possible that you believe you'll never smile again. Or sigh with relief. You're wrong my dearest Reader. But too often in this frenzied world, letting go of life's baffling circumstances in which we were hurt, betrayed, bamboozled or left holding the bag for someone else's dirty tricks is difficult, even impossible. We feel so mistreated, angry, wronged and helpless to defend ourselves. The idea of moving on to make positive choices and changes which bring about financial serenity and solvency seems beyond our strength and faith. Doesn't anyone understand? Yes, I do.

That is why distractions, encouragement and above all, cozy contentment, are all close at hand. Heaven, is too.

The 19th century New Zealand writer Katherine Mansfield reassures us: "Everything in life that we really accept undergoes a change." In my life, especially as I've been struggling financially, I have found this wisdom to be so true, it often seems miraculous. It isn't that acceptance immediately alters our conditions, punishes the bad guys and we win the lottery that night. (Although that wouldn't be a bad day, actually.) However, accepting the facts of our circumstances stops the exhausting struggle and fraught downward spirals that always hover while we attempt to find financial equilibrium. Gratitude in any form hushes the frantic energies swirling about us; and we realize that at this moment, that we have a choice: to look for the blessings or continue to make ourselves sick with worry.

By seeking the blessings we can experience a few moments of peace that quiets down the wants and lets us reclaim all the good in our lives through palpable pleasures.

Do you know the *Serenity Prayer* by the American theologian and scholar Reinhold Niebhur (1891-1971)? It was made famous by members of Alcoholics Anonymous who adopted it in the 1950s, but only the first verse. According to Niebhur, who was asked about the prayer in an interview with the *New York Times* (July 12, 1942), it had been created as part of a sermon he gave during the Great Depression:

> *God, give us Grace to accept with serenity*
> *the things that cannot be changed.*
> *Courage to change the things*
> *which should be changed*
> *and the Wisdom to distinguish*
> *the one from the other.*
>
> *Living one day at a time,*
> *Enjoying one moment at a time.*
> *Trusting that You will make all things right.*

Notice that in the first sentence, acceptance is necessary before serenity and that enjoying one moment at a time is the secret to living one day at a time with calm and contentment. We're not just surviving, we're learning to thrive in a hostile environment, like a plant, and "to thrive" is the original meaning of the word "thrift." We can trigger this inner shift, when we begin to trust that Heaven will make all things right. When we keep calm and carry on. But we need to tend this secret garden, and prime the well of our parched soul and famished heart.

I know that peace, plenty and pleasure is the last thing you think you'll ever have again in your life, which is why keeping a *Well-Spent Moments Journal* helps you acknowledge the bounty of blessings that are waiting for us every day. After just a few weeks, you'll suddenly realize you have a different kind of wealth —well-being— that's simply abundant with the small things that protect and nurture your fragile sense of faith.

Over the coming year, I want to ask you to find or create just one well-spent moment a day. Here are some examples of well-spent moments from my own journal to give you an idea of the contentment that accrues interest. And remember, all I'm asking you to do is notice, create, enjoy or prepare for one simple pleasure a day. Now write it down!

- *Music reaches beyond the barriers of our conscious mind and is a powerful ally for inner work. Gradually building a personal collection of different music selections helps you collect your thoughts, calms you down, channels your creative energy, and calls forth both peace and the sensation of plenty.*

- *Listen to your favorite music, especially if you haven't listened to it for a while. Don't multi-task, don't read, just listen. Ask yourself why this music speaks to you on such a deep level. Does it make you dream, or cry, or feel energized?*

- *Keep the radio tuned to a classical station for an afternoon. See if you can note a new piece of music to add to your list of musical pleasures.*

- *Read yourself a wonderful bedtime story, tucked under the covers with a hot milky drink. If you don't have a bedtime story that you loved as a child, take a creative excursion to the Children's Section of your local library and revel in all the beautiful illustrated books. Pick out a few to bring home.*

- *Listen in bed to the stillness of a snowfall or the icy sound of sleet against the window panes while you're all snug like a bug in bed especially if your feet are on a hot water bottle covered in cozy fleece. (Look for one at the drugstore). Let Mother Nature snuggle you in with a hush. Open the curtains to let the moonlight cross the floor.*

- *Change the fabric of your bed sheets according to season. Flannel or jersey for winter, cotton for spring and fall, linen for summer. Look for flea market finds of crocheted blankets, chenille bedspreads, vintage quilt tops to pair with your blankets. The tactile experience of our hands on something soft doesn't end when we turn five.*

You get the idea. All I'm asking you to do is perform one kind, nurturing, simple gesture or pleasurable task that makes you smile and was a well-spent moment which increased your serenity—and record it in your *Well-Spent Moments Journal*. On most days as we journey towards financial solvency, nothing much seems to be happening, but gradually the smallest change, the tiniest effort, the most seemingly insignificant action tips the scales in our favor. "Our consciousness rarely registers the beginning of a growth within us any more than without us," the

Victorian writer Mary Anne Evans, who wrote as George Eliot observed in *Silas Marner*. "There have been many circulations of the sap before we detect even the smallest sign of the bud."

Keeping a *Well-Spent Moments Journal* is how we bring ourselves back to life, one kind gesture at a time, no matter how much money is in our bank account.

Now you will give it a try, won't you?

----------XO--SBB----------

January

And what does January hold?
Clean account books. Bare diaries.
Three hundred and sixty-five new days,
neatly parceled into weeks, months, seasons.
A chunk of time, of life … those few first notes
like an orchestra tuning up before the play begins.

--Phyllis Nicholson
Country Bouquet (1947)

January

1
New Year's Day

_____

_____

_____

_____

Welcome the New Year with the delicious and traditional Southern supper of Hoppin' John: black-eyed peas (for luck), rice (for health), collard greens (for prosperity), baked ham, mini corn muffins and buttermilk biscuits.

2

_____

_____

_____

3

_____

_____

_____

Are you planning your New Year with a calendar that you love? If you haven't chosen one yet, the first week of January finds big discounts on calendars and diaries.

4

_____

_____

_____

_____

January

5

_____

_____

_____

_____

6

_____

_____

_____

7

_____

_____

_____

_____

8

_____

_____

_____

_____

Create a ceremonial for organizing the year ahead making note of seasonal pleasures as well as monthly obligations, weekly tasks and specific dates you want to remember.

"I am younger each year at the first snow when I see it, suddenly, in the air all little and white and moving; then I am in love again and very young and I believe everything."

--Anne Sexton, *American poet (1928-1974)*

January

Take your time to really clean your desk and surrounding areas. Have a good, old-fashioned purge listening to whatever music inspires you (and which has a beat), while sipping your favorite glass of good cheer. Get rid of every personal desk junk drawer. Treat yourself to pretty new files for the new year, and create a place for everything you use regularly. The well-spent investment of several hours or even a day, will pay you back with serenity for the next twelve months. How much time we squander looking for misplaced things!

For once, set aside the time to pack up the Christmas decorations properly. Mark special boxes for holiday books, DVDs, CDs and Advent Calendars marked "ADVENT." Store this box in front, so that it is the first one you see and can be easily retrieved on the day after Thanksgiving. Organization is thrilling!

9

_____

_____

_____

10

_____

_____

_____

11

_____

_____

_____

12

_____

_____

_____

January

13

_____

_____

_____

_____

14

_____

_____

_____

_____

15

_____

_____

_____

_____

16

_____

_____

_____

_____

After a lifetime of making New Year's Resolutions which are rarely achieved, try something different this year: aspirations. What pleasure would you like to introduce into your life and daily round? Don't go on a diet, do make a promise to eat as healthily as you can and increase your effort to move more.

Carve out an Artist of the Everyday surface (or even large lidded basket) to store your artist supplies. Honor your creative yearnings. If you organize a personal craft space, drawing desk, or collage tabletop with all your supplies neatly tucked away in their own marked containers, you are acknowledging to the Great Creatrix and yourself the sacredness of your artist's calling.

January

Aprons are marvelous, simply magic wands for instant role changes and beating procrastination. Collect fetching, comfortable and useful aprons (lots of pockets) for your different activities: an apron for the Inner Chef, the Homemaker, a purposeful smock for when you're creating, and a gardening apron. It may sound eccentric but when I put on the appropriate apron for the next task, my brain and resistance happily go along with me.

17

18

19

20

January

21

_____

_____

_____

22

_____

_____

_____

23

_____

_____

_____

24

_____

_____

_____

The Victorian English custom of "Keeping Winter" asks only that we acknowledge the blizzard and our natural limitations. Mother Nature's taking a nap and so should we. Slow down to enjoy the wealth and wonder of warm things that are surrounding you--the radiator heat, just baked biscuits with melted butter, a fleece covered hot water bottle at the foot of the bed. Throwing another log on the fire. The stack of logs in the basket! Fire starters that really work. Long matches. Reaching for the sweater you love and putting on the cashmere socks you got for Christmas.

January

"Year by year the complexities of this spinning world grow more bewildering and so each year we need all the more to seek peace and comfort in the Joyful Simplicities…"

Woman's Home Companion

December 1935

A hot shower after being in freezing weather. Lingering in the steam and letting the conditioner stay on a few minutes longer while you massage your aching shoulders with the pulsating water.

25

_____

_____

_____

_____

26

_____

_____

_____

27

_____

_____

_____

_____

28

_____

_____

_____

January

29

_____
_____
_____

30

_____
_____
_____

31

_____
_____
_____
_____
_____
_____

When was the last time you savored: Hot porridge with warm maple syrup; Pancakes with orange flavored sugar; Hot cinnamon buns from the oven; Café au lait; spiced cocoa; pre-lunch mugs of consommé; lemon verbena tea, glass tumblers of glogg; hot buttered rum or hot whiskey toddies resplendent with lemon and cloves, guaranteed to cure what ails you.

"Winter is the time for comfort, for good food and warmth, for the touch of a friendly hand and for a talk beside the fire: It is the time for home."

Edith Sitwell,
*English poet
(1887-1964)*

February

China tea, the scent of hyacinths, wood fires and bowls of violets — that is my mental picture of an agreeable February.

~~Constance Spry
English gardener and author
(1880-1960)

February

1

_____

_____

_____

_____

2

Candlemas Day in England, Groundhog Day in U.S.

_____

_____

_____

3

_____

_____

_____

4

_____

_____

_____

"It is winter proper; the cold weather, such as it is, has come to stay. I bloom indoors in the winter like forced forsythia; I come in to come out…"
--Annie Dillard
(1945-   )

If Candlemas Day be fair and bright Winter will take another flight. If Candlemas Day be cloud and rain Winter is gone and will not come again.
Old English weather rhyme

February

5

_____

_____

_____

_____

6

_____

_____

_____

_____

7

_____

_____

_____

8

_____

_____

_____

What indoor bulbs are blooming on your kitchen shelf? Most supermarkets and garden supply stores have discounted holiday bulb kits now. To create splendor in the pot, mix daffodils, tulips, crocus (whatever is reduced in price and sorry looking in its leftover Christmas packaging) and plant them all in one pot — you'll have a riot of color and fragrance by the end of the month.

Enjoy your evenings by candlelight. Just lighting a candle slows us down. This is the traditional week to organize your candle supply, matches and holders. Ideally store them in one basket, on one easy to reach shelf of your scented linen cupboard. But a utility room shelf will do, as long as you can find your candles and matches, if necessary, in the dark.

February

9

_____

_____

_____

_____

Assembling home-made
valentines and greeting cards
throughout the year,
gift both the sender and
receiver with pleasure. With
computers and craft sources
there are so many ways
to make this hobby both
practical and creative.

10

_____

_____

_____

_____

11

_____

_____

_____

_____

12

_____

_____

_____

_____

Raid your craft and fabric
scraps for anything red and
pink: ribbon, rick-rack,
bias tape. Now add white
lace, paper doilies, stickers,
ink stamps, double sided
tape, small sharp scissors
and pinking shears. This
would be a great time to
organize a "thinking of you"
card making tool chest which
includes an assortment of
blank envelopes and stamps.

February

13

_____

_____

_____

_____

14

St. Valentine's Day

_____

_____

_____

15

_____

_____

_____

_____

16

_____

_____

_____

_____

If you've ever run dry of DIY inspiration, for a creative excursion, cruise up and down the aisle of Michaels. It will either inspire or terrify you. It did both to me. Usually I recommend weekly creative excursions as solo dates, but for all craft and scrapbook supply stores, better be safe than sorry; take along a designated grownup girl friend with a calculator; keep cash for your purchases, a bottle of water and a vial of Rescue Remedy.

Children of all ages and their mothers, will enjoy the simple pleasure of having a "Seasonal Table" to decorate each month. Creating monthly tablescapes allows the scope of your imagination free reign and the reassuring journey through the year is enchanting for everyone. In winter a display of snowflake ornaments in a silver or pewter bowl with bare branches and ice blue and silver silk ribbons is restful for the eye.

February

Valentine's Day your table becomes bright with reds and pinks; pussy willows, shamrocks, colored eggs and a bird's nest announce spring; red-white-and-blue ribbons, tiny American flags, seashells and souvenirs decorate summer; while autumn leaves, mini pumpkins, little stalks of Indian corn and turkeys get us in a festive mood for Halloween and Thanksgiving. For Christmas, the Seasonal Table is a perfect place for an Advent Candle and evergreens. Most of all this adapted Victorian children's custom provides a rhythm to our comings and goings throughout the year and provides a comfort we are never meant to outgrow.

17

18

19

20

February

21

_____

_____

_____

_____

22

_____

_____

_____

_____

23

_____

_____

_____

24

_____

_____

_____

_____

A bedtime ritual for blissful mornings is to set yourself a pretty tray for your morning tea or coffee and leave it ready on the kitchen counter. Finding it waiting for you begins your day gracefully and if you really want to know what it's like to be pampered, you'll also find a clean kitchen and empty sink to greet you. It doesn't take much to make us happy and these simple perks are among those that money can't buy.

Febuary

Replace your morning toast toppings with seasonal jams, jellies and preserves. In January and February, experiment with the tartness of orange, tangerine and lime marmalades. In March, a spread of maple sugar butter is sublime; April brings the first of rhubarb and raspberries; May is fresh cherries; June's a glory with strawberries and scented honey; July seduces with peaches; August lures us with blueberries; September is the last month for blackberries and the first for apple butter; October's ripe with pears and persimmons; November's gift is cranberries and raisin conserve and December's toast is crowned with a dollop of whatever you fancy that's been put away in jewel-colored glistening jars patiently waiting on the pantry shelf for us! A wonderful custom is to bring back preserves from different places you visit during the year.

26

27

28/29 *(Leap Year)*

March

*A light exists in spring
not present in the year
at any other period —
when March is scarcely here.*

*~~Emily Dickinson,
American poet
(1830-1886)*

March

1

_____

_____

_____

2

_____

_____

_____

3

_____

_____

_____

4

_____

_____

_____

March

5

6

7

8

But how many of us have mastered the Art of Waiting? Let us try once again.

Reread your beloved childhood classics, especially on stormy wintry nights: **Nancy Drew, National Velvet, Anne of Green Gables.** *Listen to the sleet hit the window panes and the wind howl while you're wrapped tight as a snuggly bug in cozy flannel with a warm mug of Ovaltine.*

March

*I love **The Long Winter** by Laura Ingalls Wilder (1867-1957), the sixth book in the **Little House on the Prairie** series which tells of how Laura and her family were trapped for 7 months during the South Dakotan blizzard of 1880-81. Christmas eventually arrives in May when the trains can finally make it through bringing a holiday barrel with gifts and a frozen turkey but the real blessings are the family's awareness of their courage, fortitude, resilience, resourcefulness and gratitude for making it through a perilous time.*

9

10

11

12

March

13

_____
_____
_____
_____

14

_____
_____
_____

15

_____
_____
_____

16

_____
_____
_____
_____

Revive the wonderful ritual of a library book bag and a trip every two weeks. Transport yourself to another time, another place by immersing yourself in a lavishly illustrated travel or décor book. Discover the joy of short stories and essay compilations —each so absorbing, so satisfying and complete in just a few pages. Short story anthologies are great reads to carry along with you for company while, what else? Waiting!

Libraries are marvelous places to discover new-to-you magazines in specialty topics.

Load up on poetry that sets you pondering while you're pausing: Mary Oliver, Yeats, Whitman, Dickinson or any of Daisy Goodwin's brilliant poetry compilations which she's collected as "an anthology of emotional first-aid."

March

Learn to play solitaire—not as a computer game, but the real thing, with cards. Little surprise that the British name for this old game is Patience.

*Teach yourself old cooking skills. Frequently called "the Irish Julia Child", Davina Allen's riveting **Forgotten Skills of Cooking: The Time Honored Ways Are the Best**—a cookery school in a book with over 700 recipes adapting long lost techniques is mesmerizing. St. Patrick's Day is a marvelous prompt for discovering Irish ways in crafts, cookery, music and poetry. Make a Guinness Cake or Irish Soda Bread to celebrate March 17th.*

17
St. Patrick's Day

_____

_____

_____

18

_____

_____

_____

19

_____

_____

_____

20

_____

_____

_____

_____

March

21
First Day of Spring

_____

_____

_____

_____

22

_____

_____

_____

23

_____

_____

_____

24

_____

_____

_____

_____

What's your Sunday specialty, which is what they used to call "hobbies." Every woman needs something to do with her hands, her heart or her imagination to quiet down her mind that has absolutely nothing to do with earning money. Make March your stoke the embers of your passion month.   The August chapter in **Simple Abundance** revels in the variety of personal pursuits.

Enjoy a Spring Equinox (March 21) supper of fresh salmon with dill sauce, asparagus and boiled new potatoes with butter and parsley.

March

Prepare an indulgent bath basket for yourself. Include those treats you get for holidays and birthdays, but never know what to do with them: French milled soap, foaming bath gels, scented candles, a waterproof bath pillow. Depending on your mood, enjoy a glass of wine or a cup of fennel tea to sip.

Create a personalized "To Do" list master on your computer that includes work, home, chores, pets, kids, couples, personal and a special designated "You" time you can count on.

25

_____

_____

_____

26

_____

_____

_____

27

_____

_____

_____

28

_____

_____

_____

March

29

_____

_____

_____

_____

30

_____

_____

_____

31

_____

_____

_____

_____

_____

_____

*Good Heavens, we've been
busy and the month has
flown by...as Carrie Fisher
reminds us: "Waiting,
done at really high speeds,
will frequently look like
something else."*

April

April is Hope.

~~Gladys Taber
American Author
(1899-1980)

April

Nothing is more wondrous than the return of hope, as April casts a spell over our worn, weary, wintered and jaded senses. Like a green bud pushing through the frozen earth, or a narcissus bending her fragile stalk to the light, we reach for renewal and restoration.

The fragrance, feel, taste, sound, sight and wonder of hope is dazzling and intoxicating. Let's experience this gorgeous, tousled month by engaging our feminine wiles.

1

_____

_____

_____

_____

2

_____

_____

_____

3

_____

_____

4

_____

_____

_____

_____

April

5

_____

_____

_____

_____

6

_____

_____

_____

_____

7

_____

_____

_____

8

_____

_____

_____

_____

As soon as you can, fling open the windows and let fresh air circulate for as long as you can stand it. Air blankets and comforters out of windows and shake rugs out doors. No matter how much you may vacuum, you'll be amazed at how much dust and dander you can beat out of a carpet with a broom.

Take walks around your neighborhood and see what's different after so many months of hibernation. Breathe deeply to inhale the scent of spring: moist earth, hyacinth, forsythia, honeysuckle and camellias, all now starting to bloom.

April

9

10

11

12

April is the month of primroses. "Perhaps the elusiveness of primroses doubles their charm. Plant them, sow them, and they die. Then for no reason at all their golden stars will light some hidden corner," writes Phyllis Nicholson in April 1947. "Every spring we pack a picnic basket and set out with a ball of wool for bunching. If made into loose bundles the flowers travel better; I slip slices of raw potato in packing boxes to keep them fresh."

For centuries women have collected soft spring rainwater and used apple cider vinegar in their hair preparations. Simply place an open pail (underneath a rain gutter) to use on your hair after shampooing. Use one tablespoon apple cider vinegar to one cup of rainwater.

April

13

_____

_____

_____

_____

14

_____

_____

_____

_____

15

_____

_____

_____

_____

16

_____

_____

_____

_____

Next prepare an herbal tea using an herb depending on your hair color; chamomile for blonds, rosemary for brunettes, sage to darken grey, red hibiscus for red hair. Let the hot tea cool and add to the rainwater/vinegar solution. Keep the mixture in a pretty bottle.

April is the perfect sift, sort, repurpose or release month. Tackle one closet, a junk drawer, or a clutter hot-spot once a week.

April

Total immersion in an author's oeuvre is thrilling, especially when new-to-us information is now revealed as long out of print novels are reissued and appear free on-line offering us between-the-line detection. This is the perfect month to discover the work of Australian writer Mary Annette Beaucamp (1866-1941) whom the world knew as Elizabeth von Arnim, the author of **Enchanted April**, the story of four women of different ages, wealth and marital status bound only by their mutual unhappiness. Fleeing their misery and obligations in 1920s London they rent a magical villa in Portofino, Italy for one blissful month on their own and fall in love with their authentic selves and life once again.

17

_____

_____

_____

18

_____

_____

_____

19

_____

_____

_____

20

_____

_____

_____

April

21

_____

_____

_____

_____

22

_____

_____

_____

_____

23

_____

_____

_____

_____

24

_____

_____

_____

_____

*While **Enchanted April** is a frothy confection (both the novel and the film) the real reason I love it so is because Elizabeth was absolutely miserable when she wrote it, on deadline and for money. Just goes to prove that when push comes to shove, women can shift their mood. So much soul work is done in disguise, especially for ourselves.*

*You'll enjoy discovering Elizabeth's other novels: **Elizabeth and Her German Garden, Vera, The Solitary Summer** and **The Pastor's Wife.***

April

Sort through your make-up and discard what's old and dried out. Organize a place to store your make-up that's both easy to get to and a catch-all at the same time. Professional make up artists use a clear tool box or fishing tackle chest. Not pretty, but to the point.

Keep only the makeup that you wear and if you're at the crossroads when you face yourself in the mirror, why not visit a cosmetic counter for a creative excursion? All cosmetic companies have both spring and autumn lines. You really don't have to buy anything. Just offer enthusiastic gratitude and walk around to see how comfortable you feel in your new face. You'll probably be given a face chart showing what colors were used which is handy to keep.

25

_____

_____

_____

_____

26

_____

_____

_____

_____

27

_____

_____

_____

_____

28

_____

_____

_____

_____

April

29

_____

_____

_____

30

_____

_____

_____

_____

_____

_____

_____

_____

_____

Sort through your lingerie drawer especially if it's become the sock catch-all. Discard what's ratty (if you can) and anything you've never worn because it's too uncomfortable or unsuitable. I love to match my bras and panties, then organize by color and purpose; pretty, useful, sport. You can find drawer dividers at storage stores, or you can craft your own with some heavy cardboard covered with pretty contact paper. Lay down scented drawer liners on the bottom of the drawer and tuck in sachets or small bars of fragrant soap. I save guest soaps from hotels for this.

May

*It was one of those beautiful lengthening
days when May was pressing back with both hands
the shades of the morning and the evening.*

*~~Amelia Edith Huddleston Barr
British American novelist
(1831-1919)*

May

*May Day morning awakens
the ancient Celtic season
of Beltane. Traditionally,
this is the time for bringing
in the bounty of Mother
Nature's beauty. Open all
the windows of your home
this day and let the balmy
breezes freshen your intimate
spaces.*

1

May Day

_____

_____

_____

2

_____

_____

_____

3

*Earth is crammed with
Heaven this month...the days
are lengthening and simple
splendors are increasing.
Now it doesn't seem so
strange for us to carve out
an hour at home once a day
to coax contentment—to
comfort and cajole as we
move through the seasons of
the year.*

_____

_____

_____

4

_____

_____

_____

May

5

_____

_____

_____

_____

6

_____

_____

_____

_____

7

_____

_____

_____

_____

8

_____

_____

_____

_____

May honors Flora, the Goddess of Flowers. Early morning sojourns in your back garden bring serenity, beauty and reawakens a sense of wonder. Leave a white vintage handkerchief on a fully green bough at sunset and let the dew soak it overnight. For an appearance 'younger than springtime' dab your face with drops of dew for an everlasting radiance. Make this quiet interlude a daily investment in your spiritual beauty this month.

The second Sunday in May honors Mothers. Take your cue to replenish your Comfort drawer with tiny treats wrapped in pastel colored tissue papers and any gifts you might have received which will be more enjoyed on a night you have the blues.

In the same manner save cards and letters which uplift you to read whenever you need a boost.

May

This is the month that brings the desire for deep spring cleaning—emotionally and homekeeping—as our reawakening feminine creative energy slowly increases along with sunshine, birdsong, apple blossoms, budding lilacs and crisp lavendered linen and beeswax polish. Let us discover and cherish all the joys of May, one well-spent moment at a time.

"I do not know what you have been doing this morning, for my part, I have been in the dew up to my knees."
—Madame De Sevigne,
17th century French beauty

9

_____

_____

_____

_____

10

_____

_____

_____

11

_____

_____

_____

_____

12

_____

_____

_____

_____

May

13

_____

_____

_____

_____

14

_____

_____

_____

15

_____

_____

_____

16

_____

_____

_____

_____

Paper cornucopia flower baskets were the Victorian woman's choice to brighten spring door handles. To make them, cut an eight-and-a-half inch square of heavyweight colored paper, patterned wrapping, scrap book paper or vintage wallpaper. With the paper facing you, so that it forms a diamond, wrap the two points of the diamond together, overlapping them to form a tight cone shape. Spread a glue stick underneath the overlapping edge to secure the cone; clip together with a clothespin until the glue dries.

Now glue some paper doily trim around the top edge of the cornucopia. With a hole puncher, punch out one hole on each side of the top to tie a long ribbon handle (12 inches). Take a small piece of floral oasis, moisten and cover the top and sides with Lily of the Valley stalks and ferns. Good for the entire month of May.

May

May white lilac month...the type of glamour that haloes the home. Home is the refuge from the glamour of the market-place.

--Phyllis Nicholson
Country Bouquet (1941)

Now the lilac blooms invite us to create bouquets to celebrate the seasonal fortnight known as Lilac Tide, which gladdens even the bluest feminine soul and brightens the sacred space we inhabit. Renaissance beauties would add sprigs of lilac to their May baths to turn back the traces of time. Whether they grow in your garden or at the vendor's stall, please treat yourself this week to a halo for your own personal House of Belonging.

17

_____

_____

_____

_____

18

_____

_____

_____

19

_____

_____

_____

20

_____

_____

_____

_____

May

21

_____

_____

_____

_____

22

_____

_____

_____

_____

23

_____

_____

_____

_____

24

_____

_____

_____

_____

Decorate your mantle and table with boughs of greenery for your home and desk space. Make a simple wreath from twigs and leafy branches blown away by spring storms. Thank the trees for their offering. Ancient wise women during the Camelot era believed the simpler the wreath, the greater the power, with twigs of the blessed Hazel tree much sought after and one hair from each resident of the home was included in the weaving of the wreath.

We, too. should give thanks to Our Mother of Abiding Shelter. praying that you and yours be spared bad weather and harm in and to your house from unforeseen accidents, the storms of life and Nature's fury. Bless the walls that surround you, the roof that protects and floors that you stand upon. I have always had the Biblical verse on an entrance wall of my homes which reads: "As for me and my house, we will serve the Lord." (Joshua 24:15)

May

For a well-spent interlude, completely clean one part of your house each week of May--the food preparation area, the private sleeping area, the reception areas and the threshold of your comings and goings. Treat both your home and yourself with bouquets of white, pink and purple lilacs, and a meditative hour of puttering, but only after you bring order and serenity to the room. Puttering is the personal pleasure that increases contentment in our sacred spaces.

25

_____

_____

_____

_____

26

_____

_____

_____

_____

27

_____

_____

_____

_____

28

_____

_____

_____

_____

May

29

_____

_____

_____

Memorial Day Weekend, celebrate with the first cookout, bring out your white shoes, and make potato salad for the beginning of summer season.

30

_____

_____

_____

31

_____

_____

_____

_____

_____

_____

June

*I wonder what it would be like to live in a
world where it was always June.*

*~~Lucy Maud Montgomery
Canadian Author
(1874-1942)*

June

Create a collage of what you'd like your Well-Spent Summer to look like. Post it where you can see it upon wakening and closing your eyes at night. You'll be delighted and surprised by how powerful this paper dream can be in rearranging your time outs for good behavior.

The Anglo-Irish novelist Elizabeth Bowen believed that once we lose our innocence "it is futile to attempt a picnic in Eden." Perhaps. However, if you're feeling a little too sophisticated for your own good, or just stuck in a rut, a sure way to restore wide eyed wonder is to go on a picnic — in a shady lane or a park, by a lake, on a riverbank or a hillside. Some place where it's green and leafy and you can't see a satellite dish.

1

_____

_____

_____

_____

2

_____

_____

_____

3

_____

_____

_____

4

_____

_____

_____

June

5

_____

_____

_____

6

_____

_____

_____

7

_____

_____

_____

8

_____

_____

_____

_____

Splendid rewards await she who delights in the romance, ritual, custom and ceremony of the moveable feast. Women often sigh wistfully: "I wish my life could look like it was out of a magazine, just once." Well, it can, occasionally, and a picnic is one of those times. Outfitting your own picnic hamper is a charming hobby for the summer and an inspiring indulgence.

Begin with a lidded straw hamper or small suitcase; a vintage leather valise with well worn travel stickers is perfect. Now, with a hot glue gun and a cheerful oilcloth remnant, checked or floral (search on eBay) line your picnic carry-all.

June

9

10

11

12

The game is now afoot!
Search out flea market, and
antique stalls for porcelain
plates, thrill of thrift goblets,
Bakelite handled cutlery,
vintage table linens and
tea towels to use as oversize
napkins.

A charming crib quilt or a
twin size chenille bedspread
makes a lovely spread, topped
with a white damask trolley
tablecloth; these are what
all those 60 inch square
tablecloths were once for, the
ones you find abandoned in
antique shop corners, relics
of a golden age when the
sun never set on the Empire
and promptly at four in the
afternoon whether posted to
Ceylon, British Columbia,
Connecticut, Cardiff,
Canberra or Cheyenne
as the perfectly laundered
talisman of civilization
with crochet edges was rolled
into the drawing room on a
mahogany butler's trolley,
and for a half-hour, at least,
the weight of the world could
be carried by Atlas instead of
Herself.

June

13

14

15

16

An Edwardian housekeepers' tip that will change your life: roll your linens around a sturdy cardboard mailing tube — up to 6 napkins or placemats at a time (or matching sets!) and secure with a wide ribbons at each end. You may actually come across one of these former Victorian essentials looking like a fabric stuffed rolling pin. Now you know.

*For my picnic kit, I also like to add two small pillows, but you'll get carried away on your own and well you should, once you give yourself permission to swoon: think romance, ritual, reverie, retreat, respite. Think **Out of Africa, Somewhere in Time, A Room with a View**, even **Oklahoma** or **Carousel**. Admit it, you're smiling. This is precisely what a well-spent moment feels like. Savor the anticipation and the outcome will be glorious.*

June

Keep your picnic hamper near the back door so that the thought isn't a production, but rather a winsome matinee or a summer's well-spent moment.

Picnic menus: entire books have been written on the subject. However, simple food that stands up to warm weather arrives at the picnic site in better shape than elaborate courses and fragile foods which are best alfresco on the patio.

17

_____

_____

_____

18

_____

_____

_____

19

_____

_____

_____

20

_____

_____

_____

June

21

_____

_____

_____

_____

22

_____

_____

_____

23

_____

_____

_____

24

_____

_____

_____

Keep in mind that your spot, however warm or sunny, may be a bit damp, which is why a water-repellent pad, such as the liner from a sleeping bag is a brilliant notion, you clever girl. Topped by a soft plaid blanket and then your tablecloth.

Being a woman who has never traveled light has its advantages. I usually have stashed away the very thing everyone else forgets in the effort to be spontaneous. Planned spontenaity is more our vagabond style. That means (especially if there's a small entourage) paper towels, pre-moistened wipes, as well as a large plastic garbage bag for your trash.

June

Always bring along bug spray and a small first-aid kit to treat bee stings. Don't forget a light jacket or sweater, a travel umbrella, bottle opener and pocketknife. I have even added stormproof (wind and water) matches to my far-flung fantasy kit (thanks to Restoration Hardware) and I'm ready to head anywhere.

Keep in mind, never forget: always, always take a few spare bottles of water with you.

25

26

27

28

June

29

30

Make picnic days part of every summer and holiday with local food and new locales. You'll find shady nooks from Kansas to Kenya and create happy memories. Be sure to take your charming and unforgettable photographs. Assemble a picnic photograph album, mounting your digital photos on thick black paper with corner edges and sepia calligraphy. Every picnic will come to represent a priceless well-spent interlude, the faintest semblance of Eden.

Your lovingly assembled vintage picnic hamper would also be a heavenly gift for a daughter, a bride, a son's sweetheart, sister or best friend. For your best beau, search for handsome Art Deco patterns for the china.

July

*Summer weather, like being in love, is a
philosopher's stone which turns our ordinary
days to gold. But not the whole day...
for it is never the whole day, never all our
life which is transformed in any happiness,
but only the exquisite moments.*

--Nan Fairbrother
English landscape architect and writer
(1913-1971)

July

Women trust and act upon their instincts when it concerns their children's well-being, but shut down their sense of knowing when it's about their own needs, wants, pleasures and pursuits.

What do you need today?

What do you want to accomplish this week?

What one simple pleasure could you indulge in now?

What pursuit could you begin this month?

1

_____

_____

_____

_____

2

_____

_____

_____

_____

3

_____

_____

_____

_____

4

This Independence Day experiment with living by your senses. A woman has seven senses —five physical conduits and two spiritual channels —intuition or knowing and the sense of wonder.

U.S. Independence Day

_____

_____

July

5

_____

_____

_____

6

_____

_____

_____

7

_____

_____

_____

8

_____

_____

_____

Search out as traditional a July Fourth celebration as you can find. Attend a parade, a concert or fireworks display. Bring a covered dish to a community pot-luck picnic. Hang a flag, bake a blueberry cobbler. Independence Day is a state of mind.

Usually we deny our intuitive prompts for the best of intentions, which is really the worst: so you won't inconvenience anyone else, personally or professionally, by even considering what's good for you.

July

When was the last time you tasted something so delicious it made you swoon with pleasure?

Catch an intoxicating whiff?

Listen to some new music on a forgotten CD…organize your music according to moods.

Did you hear what your daughter was really saying?

What softness touches you as you sleep?

Change your sheets and spray with rosewater or lavender…

9

_____

_____

10

_____

_____

11

_____

_____

_____

12

_____

_____

_____

July

13

If ever there was a season to begin living intuitively, this is it. Sultry summer senses come alive in July — the month we can make the pursuit of happiness very personal. All the better if you're vacationing at home.

14

15

16

One day this week, don't wear a watch. See how time expands naturally when you're not keeping track.

July

17

Here's a well-spent moment. A screened in porch at the beach house of friends. Twilight. Shucking corn, sipping a margarita, sucking a lime dipped in salt. The steaks are grilling. Children are running. Dogs barking. I'm laughing. Happy. Grateful. It could be 1979, 1989, 1999, 2009. I hold close to this memory. Forever summer. Eternal bliss. What's yours? Write the details down.

18

19

*Read or re-read Anne Morrow Lindbergh's classic women's meditation **Gift from the Sea** originally published in 1954. Make a notation of the date. This practice is a wonderful and unusual type of diary*

20

July

21

22

23

24

Summer is when Mother Nature shows off, proving that the Universe is not stingy. Gardens and farmers' markets now overflow with the goodness of the earth.

Prepare something new for supper tonight based on what's fresh at the farmer's market. How about grilled vegetables with marinated goat cheese, bruschetta topped with tomato, mozzarella. basil and olive spread, peach shortcake with blackberry sauce.

July

Organize your cookbooks. Take them all off the shelf where you normally keep them and peruse them once again. Grab your favorite and keep it open on the counter so that it can inspire a different taste sensation this week.

Main dish salads are a cool and comfortable change for supper—especially if you make them convenient to serve. Prepare enough toppings for two or three days (with everyone's favorites) just like a salad bar and keep in separate plastic covered containers. This works well for fruit salads, but be sure to squeeze a little lemon juice on your chopped fruit to keep it from turning brown.

25

_____

_____

_____

_____

26

_____

_____

_____

27

_____

_____

_____

28

_____

_____

_____

July

29

_____

_____

_____

30

_____

_____

_____

31

_____

_____

_____   .

_____

_____

_____

_____

One of my favorite perks at a spa is the flavored water. Use the idea at home. In the morning, prepare pitchers of water featuring sliced lemon; another with sliced cucumbers and a third with sliced strawberries and blueberries. Keep in the refrigerator and enjoy throughout the day.

Let's hang the hammock, lay the blanket in the backyard, open the hamper, pop the cork. Bring out the wading pool, fire up the grill.

August

August is a wicked month.

--Edna O'Brien
Irish novelist
(1930-   )

August

Reckless, wanton, sultry, too hot to handle....August's breathing down your neck and it's not even noon. Hold it right there. When it's one hundred degrees in the shade and heat shimmers on the blacktop there are an abundance of well-spent moments waiting at home.

Heed the hammock's siren call to sensuous solitary sojourns: shady nooks, racy books, ice cream sodas. Discover that while distance might lend enchantment, the best part of every vacation is coming home.

1

_____

_____

_____

_____

2

_____

_____

_____

3

_____

_____

_____

4

_____

_____

_____

_____

August

5

_____

_____

_____

_____

6

_____

_____

_____

_____

7

_____

_____

_____

_____

8

_____

_____

_____

_____

Attics are great August destinations. Revisiting our past through sorting our memorabilia can be thrilling. Drag a box outside under something shady and make a pitcher of iced-tea with mint. Give yourself the gift of a couple of idle hours.

When we sort through our paper past, retrieving mementos and photographs from banged-up, battered and anonymous boxes, and place what's still precious in suitable labeled containers or albums, our sense memories are triggered. Like distant cousins at family reunions, each eager to share a recollection, the old letters, snowflake paperweights, matchbooks, and playbills can transport you immediately back to another time, another place, another you. And if they don't, then let go of them.

August

9

_____

_____

_____

_____

10

_____

_____

_____

11

_____

_____

_____

12

_____

_____

_____

August

13

_____

_____

_____

_____

14

_____

_____

_____

15

_____

_____

_____

_____

16

_____

_____

_____

Among the great joys of summer are the languid mornings when you can peek your eyes open and realize you don't have to be anywhere but in bed or on the porch with a cup of cheer and a new book.

"Only one hour in the normal day is more pleasurable than the hour spent in bed with a book before going to sleep and that is the hour spent in bed with a book after being called in the morning."
--Dame Rose MacAulay
English writer
(1888-1981)

August

Take an excursion to your local library and just roam the aisles for August's windfall. How to choose? This is a nice combination: One or two non-fiction books that will challenge your mind and introduce you to new information; a book of short stories for those interludes when you're waiting somewhere; a contemporary woman's novel and one from the past (visit www. persephonebooks. co.uk); a novel about a place you'd love to visit, whether it be the hills of Italy or colonial Boston; a classic that you want to re-read or one you wish you'd read instead of Cliff Notes when in high school (no matter when that was). Two or three mysteries —one new to you sleuth and one favorite; as many as you can find on one woman; a new to you cookbook and you are good for the month.

17

_____

_____

_____

18

_____

_____

_____

19

_____

_____

_____

20

_____

_____

_____

August

21

_____

_____

_____

_____

22

_____

_____

_____

23

_____

_____

_____

24

_____

_____

_____

_____

I love to combine the biographies with the work of the woman I'm reading. It feels so indulgent, like I'm devouring a box of fudge or saltwater taffy and being able to place her personal history between the lines of her fiction is mesmerizing.

A delightful way to travel and see new horizons from the Artic to the Amazon, without ever leaving the hammock, is to read about one woman explorer at a time, with both your imagination and your atlas at the ready. Absorb her experiences vicariously.

August

*If women explorers are new to you, three favorite collections guaranteed to bring out latent wanderlust are **Spinsters Abroad: Victorian Lady Explorers** by Dea Birkett (Oxford, England; Basil Blackwell 1989, out of print, but worth the search); **Living With Cannibals and Other Women's Adventures** By Michele Slung (Adventure Press/National Geographic Society) and **Unsuitable for Ladies** by Jane Robinson (Oxford University Press.)*

25

_____

_____

_____

26

_____

_____

_____

27

_____

_____

_____

28

_____

_____

_____

August

29

_____

_____

_____

_____

30

_____

_____

_____

31

_____

_____

_____

_____

_____

_____

Well-being isn't about the mind or body, but the soul. Well-being is how well you feel about being you. How's that going today?

Pick one kind thing to do for yourself today.

September

*Autumn…asks that we prepare for the future —
that we be wise in the ways of garnering
and keeping. But it also asks that we learn to let go
— to acknowledge the beauty of sparseness.*

*Bonaro W. Overstreet
American poet and writer
(1902-1985)*

September

September's sweet afterglow reminds us that sometimes it is difficult to distinguish between bad luck and new beginnings. Let the turning of the seasons gently instruct you in the art of accomplishment and fruitful well-spent moments. We're learning new tasks and pleasures this month and majoring in home schooling.

Here's the plan. Be willing to learning one fascinating thing each week that intrigues. Something that you've always wanted to know how to do but never got around to learning.

1

_____

_____

_____

_____

2

_____

_____

_____

3

_____

_____

_____

4

_____

_____

_____

September

5

What sounds like so much fun you can't wait to nail it?

6

7

"You're the only kind of knowledge they don't teach at any college. You're an education in yourself…"
-Harry Warren, Al Dubin
_(1938)_

8

September

9

"She listens to her own tales, laughs at her own jokes, and follows her own advice."
--Ama Ata Aidoo
_Ghanaian author
and playwright_

10

11

Can you?

Go to a party alone with contentment, not resentment.

Write a love letter to yourself.

Recite three poems.

Learn five new jokes and how to deliver them.

12

Tell a captivating story.

September

13

_____

_____

_____

_____

14

_____

_____

_____

15

_____

_____

_____

16

_____

_____

_____

Give a toast.

Accept a compliment.

Complain effectively.

Distract a child.

Calm a fear.

Disarm an adversary with wit.

Recover from criticism with grace.

Make the perfect comeback.

Offer a suggestion, instead of advice.

Belt out a torch song.

Administer CPR for both adults and children.

Stop profuse bleeding.

Dress a wound.

September

Treat severe burns.

Make a splint.

Remove a tick; soothe a bee sting; extract a splinter.

Pitch a tent.

Build a fire.

Bait a hook; catch a fish, fry it in a pan, and fillet it on the plate.

Bake a loaf of bread from scratch.

Make an apple pie.

Cook from memory. Have a week's repetoire in your head.

17

18

19

20

September

21

_____

_____

_____

_____

22

_____

_____

_____

_____

23

_____

_____

_____

_____

24

_____

_____

_____

_____

Pop a champagne cork.

Order wine in a restaurant.

Know five red and five white and what foods or moods they enhance.

Mix a perfect martini.

Prepare a soufflé.

Get the garlic smell off your hands and breath.

Throw a cocktail party.

Cook and eat an artichoke.

Give a dinner party for eight and enjoy it.

Self-exam your breast.

Buy the right-size bra.

Wrap a sarong.

Master five ways to wear a scarf…

September

25

Use a drill, choose the right screwdriver, hammer a nail and not your thumb.

Hang a picture alone.

Tie three different knots.

Thread a needle; sew on a button.

26

Program the DVD.

Swim a lap; stay afloat.

Drive in snow; handle a skid.

Read a map; give flawless directions.

27

Protect your privacy on the Web.

Play chess and two card games — One naughty, one nice.

28

Master Poker and Bridge and you'll never be lonely.

Know three after-dinner party games, other than Charades.

September

29

30

Place a bet, roll dice.
Shoot pool, play billiards.
Throw a dart, land a punch.

Serve an ace, swing a bat,
bowl a strike, dribble a ball,
make a Basket, sink a putt.

Saddle, mount and ride a
horse.

Understand the etiquette of
watching ball games.

Learn how to watch a
tennis match.

Master the difference between
soccer and football; cricket
and baseball.

Learn how to watch polo.
Behave well at a gaming
table.

Strike up a conversation with
a stranger; Keep up your end
of it.

Ask three interesting
questions.

Flirt with a stranger across a
crowded room.

October

October is a symphony of permanence and change.

--Bonaro W. Overstreet
American author, poet and psychologist
(1902-1985)

October

Do you know how to make God laugh? Try telling Her your plans.

Is there anything women love to do more than making plans? We organize from the inside out, careen from the right brain to the left side of the calendar, prioritize from top to bottom. Don't you get a thrill when you pick up a pen and crisp yellow ruled legal pad? Of course, you do. Because planning reinforces the feminine fantasy that we are "in control."

Ha! And then what happens? Life — that series of unexpected seemingly unconnected events — ricochets right through our reasonably well-thought out schedule. Of course, being the glorious women we are, we rise to the unexpected with as much grace as we can muster.

1

_____

_____

_____

_____

2

_____

_____

_____

3

_____

_____

_____

4

_____

_____

_____

_____

October

5

_____

_____

_____

_____

6

_____

_____

_____

_____

7

_____

_____

_____

_____

8

_____

_____

_____

_____

Heaven forefend that you might have to evacuate your home due to fire, flood, earthquake or anything else that "happens to other people."

Here's our list to enable you to "keep calm and carry on" with just an hour a day of sifting, sorting, gathering and labeling in clear plastic stacking boxes with lids, ready to be thrown into the car in case of an emergency we all know will arrive someday.

First-Aid kit.

Lanterns (4), flashlights, assorted sizes of Batteries.

Candles (4 dozen) practical candlesticks or Votive candle holders; stormproof matches; battery operated "flameless" candles or string of lights.

Battery operated shortwave radio. Store batteries with it.

October

Blankets; collapsible camp stools; sleeping bags with waterproof liner (one for every member of your family.) If there's only one of you, eventually provide for 4 people.

Toilet necessities (toilet paper, baby wipes, hygienic hand gel, diapers, poisepads, tampons.) Provide for babies, young women, as well as well as older women.

Bottles of water for drinking and washing. Eventually you want enough for a month on the move.

Emergency water-purifying tablets for 100 liters.

Canned or freeze dried food supplies; Enough for a week, eventually a month.

9

_____

_____

_____

10

_____

_____

_____

11

_____

_____

_____

12

_____

_____

_____

October

13

_____

_____

_____

_____

14

_____

_____

_____

15

_____

_____

_____

16

_____

_____

_____

_____

Long-life milk, powdered
milk and juice boxes.

Instant coffee, tea bags, hot
chocolate.

Camp stove; coffee pot, tea
pot, saucepan, skillet.

Plastic garbage bags,
assorted sizes and paper
towels.

Assorted snacks in a plastic
tub with top.

Small toys for children
(only used in emergency
situations so they will be
amusing and distracting.)

Travel edition games for
grown-ups and a pack of
cards.

Books for all ages and
inclinations; one per person.

October

Pet supplies including a leash for dogs and pet carrier, for cats (a separate one from the one lost in the garage.) If you have house cats have reserve collars and ID tags.

17

_____

_____

_____

_____

18

_____

_____

_____

_____

19

Kitty litter and rock salt stored in bucket with an ice scraper and small shovel.

_____

_____

A change of clothing for each family member, including sweatshirts and insulated vests, labeled and kept in clear plastic tub with tops.

_____

20

_____

Color-coded towels for each family member.

_____

_____

October

21

_____

_____

_____

_____

22

_____

_____

_____

23

_____

_____

_____

24

_____

_____

_____

_____

Pocket-size personal toiletries, including travel toothbrush, toothpaste, dental kits for emergency fillings (available at drug stores.)

Extra prescription medications (ask family Doctor about a special Rx for this). Regularly used over-the-counter drugs. Extra eyeglasses on chain.

Whatever it is you think you can't live without (my list includes rosary beads and 6 bottles of Rescue Remedy and my framed KEEP CALM AND CARRY ON reminder.)

October

Oh yes, and smelling salts because you're probably swooning from the very thought of this activity. That's why you're doing it in a deliberate manner, all month long.

The time you invest in "preparing" to handle any contingency you can think of is not time you're worried about money but investing in serenity. You probably have most of these items strewn around the house in various places, except the batteries. Nobody ever has enough batteries.

25

_____

_____

_____

26

_____

_____

_____

27

_____

_____

_____

28

_____

_____

_____

October

29

_____

_____

_____

_____

30

_____

_____

_____

_____

31
Halloween

_____

_____

_____

_____

_____

_____

You'd be right in thinking that outfitting our Pre-Caution Closet has been influenced by Scarlet O'Hara and Mrs. Miniver, but most of all inspired by the Bible's description of God's perfect woman in Proverbs 31:10-31, Particularly verse 21: "She is not afraid of snow for her household", especially because it only snows in the Holy Land about once every fifty years.

"It is seldom in life that one knows that a coming event is to be of crucial importance."
Anya Seton
(1904-1990)

November

The love of bare November days
Before the coming of the snow...

--Robert Frost
Pulitzer Prize winning American poet
(1874-1963)

November

November loves the pilgrim soul in you and longs to erase the fretting from your frazzled face and world-weary heart. With the holidays fast approaching, have you already grumbled away this month's gifts of grace? Family, feasting, and frazzles might be en-route, but November knows how to take care of you with a bounty of home-grown bliss. As the daylight hours decrease and the air turns crisp, let us gather unexpected spaces of serenity: the stunning, sacred ordinary days in the simply overlooked and forgotten. Encourage your cup to runneth over with remembrance and the blessings of well-spent moments.

"Stay, stay at home, my heart, and rest.. Home-keeping hearts are happiest."
Henry Wadsworth Longfellow
American poet
(1807-1882)

1
All Saint's Day

2
All Soul's Day

3

4

November

5

_____

_____

_____

_____

Start a Thanksgiving food basket and add to it throughout the month. Every week ask each family member to select something—their favorite cereal, condiment, jam or peanut butter as well as staples. This will make for very personalized and thoughtful food giveaways that always seem to increase our pleasure at sharing our blessings.

6

_____

_____

_____

7

_____

_____

_____

8

_____

_____

_____

_____

Begin to think and speak of everyday thrift as a "beauty of economy" as did our pioneer grandmothers. Victorian homemakers referred to their savings as "the margin of happiness." Reframing our money thoughts and attitudes fosters a feeling of gracious plenty rather than doing without.

November

To decorate your home, autumn's bounty is extravagant. Fill out your arrangements first with long lasting gourds, tiny pumpkins, Indian corn, wheat stalks and berries. Now stretch a small bouquet of fresh flowers in wondrous ways.

If you plan to send Christmas cards this is the week to pick them out or create a plan with the family to make cards together.

9

_____

_____

_____

_____

10

_____

_____

_____

11

_____

_____

_____

12

_____

_____

_____

November

13

_____

_____

_____

_____

14

_____

_____

_____

_____

15

_____

_____

_____

_____

16

_____

_____

_____

_____

"Everything in her surroundings ministered to a feeling of ease and amenity," wrote Edith Wharton of a woman who could choose her surroundings. We have that ability as well. Make this possibility a simple pleasure with proper lighting for reading spots, but candles elsewhere; a pillow that perfectly cradles the small of your back and a soft blanket or throw of your own.

For your Thanksgiving table blessings send "chain cards" (with a self-addressed stamped return envelope) to the members of your extended family you won't be seeing personally and ask them to recall Thanksgiving dinners past,

November

Create an autumn leaves garland of old family photographs for your table or an indoor wreath or collage in the kitchen where everyone gathers.

17

_____

_____

_____

_____

18

_____

_____

_____

_____

Rotate your family recipes to include suppers of hearty stews and soups with fresh quick breads. Cornbread, biscuits, and dinner rolls stretch food planning in such a pleasing way.

19

_____

_____

_____

_____

20

_____

_____

_____

_____

November

21

_____

_____

_____

_____

22

_____

_____

_____

_____

23

_____

_____

_____

_____

24

_____

_____

_____

_____

"November has a way of her own. Crisp air, swaying Spanish needles, echo of honking geese held in memory from the night, motors passing on the road. The secured peace of warm houses, fire and book, radio, food and light and comfort..."
--Blanche H. Dow
American Educator
(1893-1973)

November

"You say grace before meals. All right. But I say grace before the play. And the opera. And grace before the concert and pantomime. And grace before I open a book. And grace before sketching, painting, swimming, fencing, boxing, walking, playing, dancing; And grace before I dip the pen in the ink."

-G.K. Chesterton
English writer, poet, philosopher
(1874-1936)

Create a new tradition for the day after Thanksgiving that doesn't include shopping. Make a pot of turkey vegetable soup, browse through your Christmas books and magazines for a make ahead holiday dessert such as Christmas pudding, brandy or Guinness cake and prepare a grocery list, organize your holiday music and DVDs. Set the stage for a festive season.

25

_____

_____

_____

_____

26

_____

_____

_____

_____

27

_____

_____

_____

_____

28

_____

_____

_____

_____

November

29

_____

_____

_____

_____

30

_____

_____

_____

_____

_____

_____

_____

_____

_____

_____

Set aside a special space on your pantry shelf for soup fixings…stock, spices, dry beans, rice, pasta and lentils so that if you want to make soup with leftovers you can. It's very satisfying to have the ingredients for bursts of culinary inspiration. This is also a great idea for risotto. Never made risotto? Now is the time to try! You'll need Italian arborio rice.

December

December, the diamond-frosted clasp
linking twelve jeweled months to
yet another year.

--Phyllis Nicholson
Country Bouquet
(1947)

December

December's gifts —custom, ceremony, celebration, consecration--come to us wrapped up, not in tissue and ribbons, but in cherished well-spent moments. Open the gift of each day with gratitude and let the memories being made become their own season of quiet joy. Glad tidings of comfort and joy!

*Begin on December 1st to read Charles Dickens' **A Christmas Carol** aloud for just fifteen minutes an evening. Make a production out of it. Light a special candle, ring a special bell. Gather everyone around you — or if are alone, read it to yourself tucked in bed with a warm milky drink.*

1

_____

_____

_____

2

_____

_____

_____

3

_____

_____

_____

4

_____

_____

_____

December

5

_____

_____

_____

_____

Learn a new Christmas carol every week. Get the entire family involved. Host a Christmas carol fest in your home and serve mulled cider, wine and Christmas cookies.

6

_____

_____

_____

7

_____

_____

_____

Look at old photographs together and make a festive display on the wall (or a closet door) of your favorites from holidays past. Arrange them in the shape of a Christmas tree.

8

_____

_____

_____

December

Decide on toys and a care baskets for local charities. Dedicate sharing your Christmas as much as possible.

9

_____

_____

_____

_____

10

_____

_____

_____

11

Create a simple ornament and date it and make one for every member of the family.

_____

_____

_____

12

_____

_____

_____

December

13

_____

_____

_____

_____

Go through your collection of ornaments and then act as a "curator" of your Christmases past by recording a story about each ornament.

14

_____

_____

_____

15

_____

_____

_____

_____

16

_____

_____

_____

Take a trip down memory lane with displays of fir branches, paper chain garlands, tinsel (if you don't have pets) and ornaments from the past (vintage or reproduction.) Remember "bubble" ornaments. Visit www.vermontcountrystore. com for all your nostalgia desires.

December

Green boughs tucked behind pictures and on shelves is a Victorian tradition. Hang mistletoe boughs over the doors of all bedrooms.

17

_____

_____

_____

_____

18

_____

_____

_____

_____

19

_____

Victorian families decorated "feather trees," but large branches spray painted white with glitter, arranged in a sturdy vase, make a stunning display. If you add tiny stockings it can become an Advent calendar.

_____

_____

20

_____

_____

_____

December

21

_____

_____

_____

Really write a letter to Santa Claus! Write a thank you note to Heaven! Make this an annual tradition and your family will treasure this custom.

22

_____

_____

_____

23

_____

_____

Go through your old family Christmas recipes. Select a few and make out your ingredient list and make a date in your holiday calendar to prepare them.

24

Christmas Eve

_____

_____

_____

December

Write it down,
when I have perished;
Here is everything
I've cherished;
That these walls
should glow with beauty,
Spurred my lagging soul
to duty;
That there should be
gladness here
Kept me toiling,
year by year.
Every thought and every act
were to keep this home intact.
--Edgar A. Guest
English born American poet
(1981-1959)

Can you allow yourself to
enjoy Christmas this year?

This is my Christmas wish
for both of us: that behind
the toys, tinsel, carols, cards,
and convivial chaos, there will
come a moment of reflection
and peace. May it be said of
each of us that we know how
to keep Christmas well, if any
woman does.

Merry Christmas! And God
bless us everyone!

25
Christmas Day

_____

_____

_____

_____

26

_____

_____

_____

_____

27

_____

_____

_____

_____

28

_____

_____

_____

_____

December

29

30

31
New Year's Eve

What are you doing New Year's Eve? Hopefully, preparing your heart for the mystical turn of tide and time.

However, before we can welome in the New Year, we need to put the Old Year's unfinished business—mistakes, regrets, shortcomings, and disappointments—behind us.

Here's how; write down on small slips of paper whatever you'd like to forget and put in a small cardboard box. Next with ceremony, wrap the box in black or very dark paper, sealing in the sorrow and hard luck. Say, "Good Riddance," and toss the box into the fireplace or in a grill to burn away the past. If you don't have a fireplace, toss the box into the trash where they belong. Keep only the good.

Chill something bubbly. Honor the Old Year with a farewell, then welcome the New Year within.

Fifty Overlooked Occasions to Create Well-Spent Moments

There are no little things. "Little things,"
so-called, are the hinges of the universe.
--Fanny Fern
(1870)

Every time your husband or partner returns home, rise to greet them with a hug and a kiss.

Time you spend on the phone with your busy daughter or daughter-in-law.

The surprise phone call to faraway family and friends.

Placing family pictures on the wall so that everyone can see them and know they are loved.

Touching your grown children on the back to acknowledge they have your full attention while their little ones are vying for your attention, too.

Telling family stories to the youngest child so that he knows what came before him.

Creating a ritual which involves the in-laws, such as gathering at your mother-in-laws house on a Sunday for the men to prepare dinner as they watch football and the women sit and chat.

The time you spent biking, swimming and picnicking—playing—with you grandchildren is the heart's favorite investment.

After you spend time with your children or grandchildren typing up their stories in a continuing journal celebrating the "ordinary" days.

When giving someone a book, taking the time to write something in the cover of how this book was chosen for them.

On holidays whose origins have been forgotten, see if you can create a living link. For example Memorial Day weekend in May began because Southern women were decorating the graves of their lost Confederate sons. But when they looked over to where the Union soldiers were buried, they noticed that no one was tending the Union graves and so they did. Create a new-to-you Memorial tradition to go to your family's grave site and tend it together. This custom allows you to reflect on the memories of those who have gone before us, and remember the wonderful lives they led and the lessons they taught as a new bud and leaf on your family tree. This is particularly soothing if you still feel estranged from family members who died before reconciliation.

On Labor Day weekend, trace the historical tree of your family's work history.

When traveling, if you see a soldier in uniform, take the time to stop him or her and thank them for their service. If you're ahead of them in a coffee line, try to pay for them, if you can. The smile, surprise and genuine delight in this exchange makes this a very well-spent moment.

Enjoy the weather changes in a small ceremonial – when a thunderstorm is rolling in, stay on your porch or in the house and enjoy the Mother Nature firework like light show. I love to cuddle in bed when the snow is falling — it sounds so silent — but in my imagination it becomes another layer of downy Divine protection.

Some of us are lucky to be able to revisit where we grew up, or our family still lives there. These childhood memories are powerful links to our well being today. If you have a hankering to go visit your grandmother's old homestead, then make plans to do so.

On secret anniversaries of the heart, it's fun to prepare foods that you remember enjoying with someone special. My Mother will always be a part of me with her special meal; soup beans (pinto beans), mashed potatoes, coleslaw, cornbread and a cold beer. Corned beef with cabbage for St. Patrick's Day plucks my Irish sentimentality.

Re-instate (if they've ever fallen away) particular meals and memories. You love to bake cinnamon rolls for your son; I love surprising my daughter with hot croissants; or you remember chipped beef on toast as the meal your family had every Sunday after church, while vying for the comics.

Guess who's coming to dinner? Choose one day a week to dress up your table for a beautiful meal. I used to do this on Sunday, after a visit to the local farmer's market. What happy memories this brings. Those were the best meals.

If you're able have a set of breakfast dishes—sunny, cheery and happy— which can be amusingly put together with flea market finds; and while you're at it, gather a special dinner set with plate, cutlery and linen napkins you've sourced at vintage shops.

Create several sacred spaces for yourself. One in your house, perhaps a comfortable chair with a reading light that looks over a garden and one outside in the city where you live. Create an altar of intentions and prayers that hold objects that are sacred to you. Find a spiritual garden within walking distance. Mine used to be a walled herb garden on the grounds of the National Cathedral in Washington, D.C..

In your town or city, see if there is a Buddhist temple or Japanese tea garden (no matter what your religious affiliation) because there you will find simple and soulful ideas for renewable (to your spirit) gardening.

If you don't have cats, place a birdfeeder near your deck or patio and enjoy watching them. If you do have cats, don't place the feeder where the cats have access to the birds, but do call a time out for a cup of tea or coffee whenever your cats are engaged in play. It's only for a few minutes but the break lowers your blood pressure and heightens your ability to smile.

Whenever you and your husband are watching television or a movie together (especially if it's a chick flick) give him a loving head, foot, neck or shoulder massage.

Let your animals curl up with you. One of my little kittens starts mewing early in the day for her place on my chest, nesting her little paws on the bedspread. It's a riot to watch, and it makes me so happy for her companionship and the knowledge that at the end of the day, there's a good book, something wonderful to sip, and Maggie Grace purring in the crook of my neck.

Create one-on-one time with each child and grand-child, so they get to know you personally and more importantly you get to know and listen to them. We never know the moments that we will come to cherish in our lives, but I'd be willing to bet the farm that one of your and my most golden memory is time with our children.

Tape stories aloud –books you've loved, memories you have, and capture them on video and audio for your loved ones.

Movie theme nights are fantastic. Pair music, movie and the meal. Enjoy Mexican enchiladas with chocolate mole sauce while watching the sensuous *Like Water for Chocolate* or chocolate mousse which watching *Chocolat*; Chinese carryout to accompany the delectable feast *Crouching Tiger, Hidden Dragon*; tea and crumpets with *Miss Marple*.

Filling a basket with colorful violets, pansies or herbs and delivering it to a person who needs a spiritual lift, anonymously will endow you in a tremendous glow of gratitude that brightens even the gloomiest of days.

Moments spent learning a new feature on the digital camera, reading about an investment strategy, figuring out how to add extra antioxidants to my diet or researching the controversy over who really wrote Shakespeare's plays pay dividends on how fulfilled your day, week or month seems. Home schooling in the age of the internet is investing in yourself.

Learning to do yoga, then making a commitment to a yoga session a week is committing to your health: mind, body, spirit.

Sign up for some kind of movement class — Pilates, dancing, Zumba fitness classes, even walking will help you feel better within a short period of time. It's the getting over the seat of your pants resistance that's the challenge.

If your surroundings have you in the dumps, schedule a creative excursion to a large home improvement warehouse. Cruising the aisles and discovering a paint chip in the shade of Wedgewood blue or pale Daffodil can be all the motivation you need.

Create a wall sized mood board. Find a blank wall or closet door in your private areas for an inspiration collage of fabrics, furniture styles, paint chips, pictures that speak to you and put them all where you can see them morning and night. Let yourself add a new picture everyday. Do this for a month and then ask yourself what you should be doing with your life (if you wonder), where should you live, are you happy in your relationship, what you need more of (romance, spontaneity, mystery.)

If you've been down in the dumps, rise early enough to watch the sun come up and linger with a sunset wherever you can find it. There is solace in the ancient dance of continuity.

Indulge in period films—take one era at a time. The Movie Channel is a treat resource (www.tcm.com) Search the web for Film Noir sites and www.enchantedserenityofperiodfilms.com, a wonderful blog with an enormous range of information.

Setting a time for solo prayer and meditation is important, but praying with your partner and children even if it's just grace before meals is amazing. Remember Meister Eckhart who said, "If the only prayer you ever say is 'thank you,' it will be enough."

A spontaneous dance to a song you love.

Waiting in the car, even after you've arrived someplace to hear the end of a song you're enjoying.

Savoring the first sip of tea or coffee in the morning.

Taking deep breaths and giving thanks for your healthy body.

Making your end of day soak or shower luxurious in the time you allow yourself, the fragrance of your soap or bathing gel, the softness of your towel, the cuddle factor of your robe. Now place a large towel on your bed and just lay down for five minutes.

Warming up a towel in a dryer for someone you love as they take a shower (this could include you!)

Being near the water—ocean, lake, water fall, fountain or window during a rain storm just to listen to the rhythm of water.

Using your hands for a craft project.

Finding a new craft project that excites you and creating a ritual at least once a week to integrate it in your daily round.

Writing notes of encouragement – in a card or on a Post-It note and leaving it where it will be found and treasured.

Stargazing as often as you can. Prepare a stargazing basket with a blanket, a flashlight and a telescope if you have one. You don't? Not to worry Astronomy books and maps are a great place to start. My favorite book is *The Backyard Stargazer* by Patricia Price.

Making a wish and believing in it until it comes true. In the new year, I'm trying an experiment with the universe: Wishing. I'm using as my two guides *The Wishing Year: A House, A Man, My Soul—A Memoir of Fulfilled Desire* by Noelle Oxenhandler (Random House) and *Wishing: How to Fulfill Your Heart's Desires* by Elizabeth Harper (Atria Books).

Try an experiment in order to ransom back some of your time as well as your soul over the weekend. Declare the weekend as a shopping free zone and get everything you need for your weekend on Thursday. Use your two shopping free days to simply recharge your physical batteries and have fun. Take a deep breath and smile; I know these are *new* concepts to take in.

Begin with a "Quiet Night In" on Fridays, shared with yourself and specifically invited others (if necessary) but my Quiet Night In is exactly that. Solo. Me and a little Night Music. Here is the making of it: something delicious to read (a book or magazine), something tasty and comforting to eat while propped on the couch or in bed watching a new DVD and something scrumptious to drink that makes you feel festive from the first sip. My favorite Friday night supper is a Big Girls Nibble Plate: good thin, Italian salami, cheese (a garlic soft cheese), a small slice of pate, Dijon mustard, Greek olives stuffed with blue cheese, cornichons (small sour green pickles) that go with pate; and a loaf of fresh French bread—all washed down with copious amounts of Voss sparkling water and a bottle of pinot noir.

Saturday can be a day devoted to visit something you really want to see: an exhibition, a concert, a movie, or a class that you're taking. It's nice to designate Saturday night as a pot luck supper and invite a few friends around, each bringing part of the meal: appetizer, main dish, salads/breads and dessert. I'm always astonished at the pleasure this brings.

Elevate Sunday to its proper place in the full panoply of the seven days making up the Divine Week. Beginning with a blessed sleep in—ordained by Mother Plenty to soothe the ragged edges of your soul, followed by a leisurely and scrumptious breakfast late enough to become brunch and serve a menu that is usually only reserved for special occasions: Eggs Benedict, French Toast, Blueberry pancakes, pumpkin spice bagels and orange marmalade cream cheese—you get the idea.

Designate an "Hour a Day" at home for whatever you want it to mean and however you want to spend it. It could be an hour's unwinding at the end of the busy day, an hour to focus on some of your little "To Do" projects to make your house more livable, or it could be an hour for you to do nothing, but sit in a big chair after dinner over peppermint tea and work for just one hour on your needlepoint project. The beauty of you deciding how to use your hour at home, is a well-spent indulgence that lays the groundwork for a life of your own. Imagine 7 hours a week, for you to do something at home for pure pleasure. Every time you begin to feel nervous about money, or the future, remind yourself of your private account—your accumulation of Well-Spent Moments—cherished by you, for you to help reinforce your "Margin of Happiness."

Blessings on your creativity, courage and moxie.

Dearest Love,
Sarah Ban Breathnach

With Thanks and Appreciation

It isn't the great big pleasures that count the most;
It's making a great deal out of little ones.
--Jean Webster, **Daddy-Long-Legs**
American writer
(1876-1916)

Many thanks and much appreciation to our **Simple Abundance** and **Peace and Plenty** Certified Leaders who enthusiastically spread the good word on my behalf. A particular bow of gratitude to Mary Jane Hurley-Brant, Bonnie DeMartini, Kathy Zehringer, Deborah Johnson, Mary E. Knippel, Jessica Kolterman, Linda Lenore, Debra Letton, Betsy Malloy, Shelly A. Munoz, Melanie Raffaelli, Martha Tait-Watkins for sharing their personal Well-Spent Moments with us.

And a special note of thanks to the **Simple Abundance** Executive Director, my sister, Maureen O'Crean who is our cheerleader, confidant and my constant source of amazement, appreciation and inspiration, for keeping us all together and rowing in the same direction, through storms, past shoals to safe harbor on her Good Watch.

May peace and plenty always be their well-deserved portions.

Blessings on our courage.

Dearest Love,
Sarah Ban Breathnach

Please visit us and join our
online community at
www.simpleabundance.com

CPSIA information can be obtained at www.ICGtesting.com
Printed in the USA
BVOW051551030413

317156BV00008B/235/P